Permanent Deacons

in the United States

Guidelines on Their Formation and Ministry

1984 Revision

Bishops' Committee on the Permanent Diaconate
National Conference of Catholic Bishops

In its planning document, as approved by the general membership of the National Conference of Catholic Bishops in November 1984, the Bishops' Committee on the Permanent Diaconate was authorized to publish the text for the revision of *Permanent Deacons in the United States: Guidelines on Their Formation and Ministry*. This present document, approved by the NCCB on November 15, 1984, is authorized for publication by the undersigned.

Monsignor Daniel F. Hoye
General Secretary
NCCB/USCC

July 29, 1985

ISBN 1-55586-974-2

Contents

Abbreviations

AA   *Apostolicam Actuositatem;* Decree on the Apostolate of the Laity, Vatican Council II.

AGD   *Ad Gentes Divinitus;* The Decree on the Church's Missionary Activity, Vatican Council II.

CD   *Christus Dominus;* Decree on the Pastoral Office of Bishops in the Church, Vatican Council II.

CIC   *Code of Canon Law.*

LG   *Lumen Gentium;* Dogmatic Constitution on the Church, Vatican Council II.

SC   *Sacrosanctum Concilium;* The Constitution on the Sacred Liturgy, Vatican Council II.

Documents Frequently Quoted

Ad Pascendum — Apostolic Letter of Pope Paul VI, August 15, 1972.

Ecclesiae Sanctae — Apostolic Letter of Pope Paul VI, August 6, 1966.

Pontificalis Romani Recognito — Apostolic Constitution, Pope Paul VI, June 17, 1968.

Sacrum Diaconatus Ordinem — Apostolic Letter of Pope Paul VI, June 18, 1967.

Preface

In its Dogmatic Constitution on the Church, the Second Vatican Council decided to restore the diaconate as a permanent order of ministers in the Church. In *Lumen Gentium*, 29, the council briefly described the nature and functions of the diaconate and the need of the Church it hoped this ministry would meet and left it to local episcopal conferences to decide, with papal approval, whether or not to restore the diaconate in their own countries.

During the next several years, Pope Paul VI implemented the council's decision in three important steps. The Apostolic Letter *Sacrum Diaconatus Ordinem* (June 18, 1967) established canonical norms for the permanent diaconate. On June 17, 1968, new rites for the conferral of all three of the ordained ministries were authorized in the Apostolic Constitution *Pontificalis Romani Recognito*. Finally, on August 15, 1972, Pope Paul VI published new norms for the diaconate in the Apostolic Letter *Ad Pascendum*.

The bishops of the United States decided in the spring of 1968 to petition the Holy See for permission to restore the diaconate in this country. In their letter of May 2, 1968, they offered the following as the reasons for their request:

- to enrich and strengthen the many and various diaconal ministries at work in this country with the sacramental grace of the diaconate;
- to enlist a new group of devout and competent men in the active ministry of the Church;
- to aid in extending needed liturgical and charitable serv-

1

ices to the faithful in both large urban and small rural communities;

- to provide an official and sacramental presence of the Church in many areas of secular life, as well as in communities within large cities and sparsely settled regions where few or no priests are available;
- to provide an impetus and source for creative adaptations of diaconal ministries to the rapidly changing needs of our society.

On August 30, 1968, the Apostolic Delegate informed the United States bishops that Pope Paul VI had acceded to their request.

The following November, the Bishops' Committee on the Permanent Diaconate was established. Its principal functions are

- to offer local bishops recommendations concerning concrete details of and questions about diaconal vocations;
- to establish a formation program including doctrinal, pastoral, and spiritual aspects of training;
- to review and approve plans for the ministry of deacons, developed by various dioceses;
- at the request of local ordinaries, to make formal evaluations of diaconal programs after they have been operating for three years.

Diocesan diaconal programs began to be developed almost immediately upon reception of permission from Rome. Within two months of its inception, the Committee on the Permanent Diaconate had received four initial proposals for training programs. By the spring of 1971, thirteen programs were in operation, with a total of 430 candidates. The first group of ordinations to the permanent diaconate took place in May and June of 1971.

Late in 1971, the committee, under the chairmanship of Bishop Ernest L. Unterkoefler, issued *Permanent Deacons in the United States: Guidelines on Their Formation and Ministry*. These guidelines drew upon the experience and knowledge gained in the initial programs and upon a report of the Catholic Theological Society of America on the theology of the diaconate. The guidelines were written in a creative and open manner and served the American Church well, as it began to assimilate the new ministry of the deacons.

Since then, the diaconate has grown remarkably in the United States. In 1971, there were 58 deacons and 529 candidates; in 1973, 411 deacons and 870 candidates; in 1975, 1,074 deacons and 2,243 candidates. By 1980, the number of deacons had quadrupled to 4,656, with another 2,514 candidates. According to the latest figures (1984), there are 7,102 deacons and 2,114 candidates. Of the 181 dioceses in this country, 142 have diaconal programs.

In February 1978, the committee was authorized to commission a comprehensive study of the permanent diaconate in the United States. The results of that survey were published in 1981, under the title *A National Study of the Permanent Diaconate in the United States*. This volume points up the strengths and weaknesses of the diaconate as it has developed in this country and makes suggestions for improving formation programs and for the exercise of this ministry in the Church.

The National Conference of Catholic Bishops now publishes these revised guidelines to refine the vision expressed in the 1971 guidelines, in the light of experience. They are motivated by the fact that the earlier guidelines were produced from a wish to assist the establishment of the diaconate in this country but could not reflect actual experience, since they were written before any permanent deacons were ordained. They have also been motivated by the concern of diocesan bishops that existing formation and ministerial efforts be corrected, improved, and updated in light of increased theological understanding and ecclesial practice.

While the survey noted above provided empirical data gathered by a professionally organized national research project questioning bishops, supervisors, deacons, and the wives of deacons, the process of drafting these present guidelines provided further consultation and data. A first draft was prepared during the summer of 1983, and was discussed by the Committee on the Permanent Diaconate, under the chairmanship of Bishop John J. Snyder. Also present were personnel from the USCC Office of Research and officers of the National Association of Permanent Diaconate Directors. On November 13, 1983, the committee approved the draft for circulation to elicit feedback. It was sent to every bishop and diocesan director of the diaconate, with an instrument to guide consultation of all deacons, wives of deacons, priests, religious, and laity involved with the diaconate. This material was returned to the Office of Research by March 15, 1984, for processing and then given to the authors of the draft for revision of the material. The second draft was discussed by the committee, under the chairmanship

3

of Bishop John F. Kinney, during a meeting, June 19-20, 1984. Taking an active part in the discussions were the consultors, offices, and organizations present at the November 13, 1983, meeting noted above. With additional emendations, the draft was accepted by the Committee on the Permanent Diaconate on June 20, 1984, and forwarded to the NCCB Administrative Committee, requesting that it be transmitted to the general membership of the National Conference of Catholic Bishops for action and publication.

Gratefully conscious of those who have served on the Committee on the Permanent Diaconate, particularly of the guidance of Bishop Ernest L. Unterkoefler, who served as chairman at the time of the original publication of the guidelines, the National Conference of Catholic Bishops also acknowledges the direction of Bishop John J. Snyder, under whose chairmanship the present effort was begun, and Bishop John F. Kinney, under whose chairmanship it has been brought to this conclusion. Appreciation is also expressed to Msgr. Ernest J. Fiedler, former director of the Secretariat of the Committee on the Permanent Diaconate, and Rev. Joseph A. Komonchak, consultor to the committee, who together prepared the drafts of the text; Deacon Samuel M. Taub, staff associate to the committee; and Mrs. Kathleen Murray and Mrs. Dorothy Titman, who provided the secretarial assistance.

Chapter I

The Deacon in the Ministry of the Church

A. MINISTRY AND MINISTRIES IN THE CHURCH

1. When the Second Vatican Council decided to restore the diaconate as a permanent ministry in the Church, it did so as part of its renewed vision of the Church. Since an understanding of the ministry depends on an understanding of the Church, it is necessary to review briefly the central features of the council's vision of the Church, before the diaconate itself can be described and understood. This chapter, then, will prepare for a description of the diaconate by discussing the role of the whole Church as the sacrament of salvation, the realization of the mystery of the Church in local communities, the common part all Christians have in the life and activity of the Church, and the special role of the ordained ministry.

1. The Church as the Sacrament of Christ

2. The Church is the People of God, the Body of Christ, and the Temple of the Holy Spirit.[1] It is at once "a community of faith, hope, and love" and "a visible organization"; "a society structured with hierarchical organs and Jesus Christ's Mystical Body; a visible social group and a spiritual community; an earthly Church and a Church endowed with heavenly gifts."[2] This

---

1. LG 17.
2. LG 8.

5

messianic people, "established by Christ as a communion of life, love, and truth, is taken up by him as the instrument of the redemption of all and is sent out by him into the whole world as the light of the world and the salt of the earth (see Mt 5:13-16)."[3] "Rising from the dead (see Rm 6:9), Jesus Christ has sent his life-giving Spirit upon his disciples and through him established his Body which is the Church as the universal sacrament of salvation,"[4] that is, "the sign and instrument of intimate union with God and of the unity of the whole human race."[5]

3.   Through his words and deeds, through his death and resurrection, and through the gift of his Spirit, Jesus Christ has established in human society and history a new reality, a community of men and women distinct from all other social bodies by their faith, hope, and love.[6] They are a community of faith because they receive the Gospel of Jesus Christ, celebrate his memory, and interpret God, the world, and the human condition in the light of his teaching, life, death, and resurrection. They are a community of hope because they live in trusting expectation of the power of Christ's Spirit and the final triumph of God's reign. They are a community of love because even now they rejoice in and celebrate the love of God that has been poured forth into their hearts and creates a communion of love among them. This "communion of life, love, and truth"[7] is the social and historical difference that Jesus Christ has meant to the world, a sign testifying by its very existence to the love of God, which is in Christ Jesus and his Holy Spirit.

4.   Precisely as the creation of God's Word and grace, the Church is simultaneously also the social and historical instrument of God's redemption of the world. In the Church, the Good News of Jesus Christ continues to be told and applied to the changing circumstances and challenges of human life; and this proclamation of the Gospel offers others the possibility of hearing about Jesus Christ and embracing his saving message. As Christians live their lives in the power of the Spirit's grace and in the assurance of God's future promise, they offer others a hope to live by, encouraging them also to resist and overcome the forces of evil, personal and social, by which they may con-

---

3. LG 9.
4. LG 48.
5. LG 1.
6. LG 8.
7. LG 9.

sider themselves bound. In the love among Christians, God continues to reconcile people to himself and to give them the power to transcend the many divisions from which they suffer. In the sacraments, which symbolize and make real again the gifts of God that are the origin, center, and goal of the Church's life, the power of Jesus Christ's redemption is again and again at work in the world. And, thus, in the communion of life, love, and service realized under the leadership of the successors of the apostles, a vision of reconciled humanity is offered to the world.

5.   The Church is thus the universal sacrament of salvation, the social and historical sign and instrument of his redemptive Word and grace. It is at once the Body of Christ, in which his Spirit dwells as in a Temple, and the People of God on mission in the world. If it displays in its life and activity the Word and grace from which it springs, the Church is already the instrument by which Jesus Christ continues to be active for the world's redemption. In this sense, the Church, as the redeemed community, is also the primary minister of Jesus Christ in the world.

2. The Local Church

6.   The Church is both one and universal. It is one in virtue of its unity of faith and love, under one God and Lord, in the one Spirit, and in the apostolic communion of the head and members of the College of Bishops. It is universal, not merely in virtue of its geographical extension, but because "each of its parts contributes its own gifts to other parts and to the whole Church, so that the whole and each of its parts are strengthened by the common sharing of all things and by the common effort to attain to fullness in unity."[8] In other words, the Church is universal, not in spite of the rich diversity of its particular realizations throughout the world, but through them and in them it is a *Catholic* Church, embracing, making its own, and transforming in Christ all that is valid in the world's many cultures. By the common faith, love, and apostolic communion, particular Churches are "constituted after the model of the universal Church"; and, in turn, "it is in them and out of them that the one and unique Church comes to be."[9]

---

8. LG 13.
9. LG 23.

7. In the many references to local or particular Churches in the council documents, two primary themes emerge: first, the common spiritual principles on which and through which the local or particular Churches are built up; and, second, the particular sociocultural conditions in which the Church comes to be.

8. Local or particular churches are not simply administrative units of the worldwide Church. According to the council, the Church is constituted by the call of God, the Word of Jesus Christ, the grace of the Spirit, and the exercise of the ministry of the successors of the apostles.[10] Where these all are found, the Church, in its full and distinctive reality, is found. Each community so gathered is the Church in a particular place, the one universal Church, realized as a concrete community of men and women in Jesus Christ. Each such community constitutes an instance of that redeemed and redemptive community that is the sign and instrument of Jesus Christ. The one universal Church is realized in them, and the communion in faith, love, and apostolic unity of such particular or local Churches constitutes the one and universal Church.

9. This specific realization of the universal Church is preeminently found in a diocese, which the council defined as "a portion of the People of God entrusted to a bishop to be guided by him with the assistance of his clergy so that, loyal to its pastor and formed by him into one community in the Holy Spirit through the Gospel and the Eucharist, it constitutes one particular Church in which the one, holy, catholic, and apostolic Church is truly present and active."[11] The council also acknowledged that "the Church of Christ is really present in all legitimately organized local congregations of the faithful, which, united with their pastors, are also called Churches in the New Testament. For in their own places, these congregations are the new People called by God, in the Holy Spirit and with full conviction (see 1 Th 1:5). In them the faithful are gathered through the preaching of the Gospel of Jesus Christ, and the mystery of the Lord's Supper is celebrated. . . . In each altar community, under the bishop's sacred ministry, a symbol may be seen of that charity and 'unity of the Mystical Body, without which there can be no salvation.' In these communities, although

---

10. See LG 26 and CD 11.
11. CD 11.

they are often small and poor or scattered, Christ is present through whose power the one, holy, catholic, and apostolic Church is brought together."[12]

10. With these statements, the council sought to emphasize that the one and universal Church is always realized in particular local communities of the faithful, under the leadership of a bishop (a diocese) or of his representative (a parish or other group of the faithful). Such communities are the Church of Christ in a particular place, the Body of Christ, and the People of God on missionary pilgrimage in the world. And, when attention is turned to these particular realizations of the Church, the sociocultural conditions within which the Church is always realized also come to our attention: the economic, social, political, and cultural circumstances in which the Word of Jesus Christ and the grace of the Spirit are communicated and received. For the Word and grace of God are never communicated and received in the abstract or in general. The community of faith arises because the one Gospel of Christ has been preached and related to the various concrete circumstances in which individuals and societies seek to give order and purpose to their lives. The community of hope arises because people suffering specific temptations to despair have been blessed by God to trust in the power of the Spirit and the coming of the Kingdom. The community of love arises when alienated and divided individuals and groups are brought together by God's love of them and by their love for one another.

11. The council strongly stressed the effort to make the Church at home in the varied cultures of the world. "Christ and the Church which bears witness to him through the preaching of the Gospel transcend the distinctions of race and nationality and therefore cannot be considered strangers to anyone or to any place."[13] Christians "must express their new life in their own society and native culture, according to the traditions of their own nation. They must know this culture, must heal and preserve it, must develop it in accord with modern conditions, and finally must perfect it in Christ, so that the faith of Christ and the life of the Church are not alien to the society in which they live, but begin to permeate and to transform it."[14]

---

12. LG 26.
13. AG 8.
14. AG 21.

12.   It is to be expected, then, that the universal Church will, in its various particular realizations, reflect the shape and texture of the sociocultural circumstances in which it arises and exists. It is a universal Church that is at the same time at home in all the regions of the world, among all ethnic groups and races; a Church for the late twentieth century, as once it was a Church for earlier centuries; one Church, because one Gospel, one Spirit, one Eucharist everywhere gather it together in communion with the head and members of the College of Bishops. It is a universal Church because everywhere that Gospel, Spirit, and Eucharist meet and respond to the particular needs and questions of individuals and societies.

3. The Common Responsibility

13.   As the sacrament of salvation, the Church as a whole is the primary social and historical instrument through which his redemptive power reaches the world. But, it can be this only if all its members assume their responsibility for the upbuilding and activity of the Church. This is a right and a duty which all members of the Church share in virtue of their baptism and confirmation and in accordance with the charisms they receive. As in the human body, so also in the Church there should be no purely passive members.[15] To each has been given some gift for the common good that carries with it the right and responsibility to use it for the good of the whole Body of Christ.[16] For all of the differentiations that exist in the Church on the basis of distinct charisms and ministries, "there remains a true equality among all with regard to the dignity and to the activity which is common to all the faithful in the building up of the Body of Christ."[17] The Church exists, lives, and acts out of the wonderful exchange by which, under grace, its members both serve one another and are served by one another.

14.   This principle must guide any theological or practical articulation of ministries within the Church. The building up of the Body of Christ and the accomplishment of its mission in the world are the effects of the activities of *all* the members of the Church. The Word that is preached to the Church, the sacra-

---

15. See AA 2.
16. See AA 3.
17. LG 32.

ments that give it life and strength, and the authority of their leaders call Christians to undertake the countless acts of daily Christian service: in conversations, in gestures of sympathy and support, in individual and communal prayer, in parents' guidance and instruction of their children, in formal activities of catechesis and teaching, in care of the sick, poor, and needy, etc. Such activities in response to grace are concrete expressions of faith, hope, and love. These acts of service are the living fiber of the Church. They both presuppose and undergird the central activities of preaching, sacramental celebration, and community guidance. They are indispensable to the concrete, everyday building up, life, and activity of the Church.

4. Ordained Ministries in the Church

15.   If every Christian has his or her own gift from the Spirit, not all receive the same gifts. In the Church there is a unity of mission and a diversity of ministry.[18] And, the Church is the healthy and living Body of Christ when all submit their gifts to the discernment of the community, acknowledge the gifts others have been given, serve as their own gifts permit, and are willing to be served by the gifts others receive.

16.   Central among the many ministerial gifts Christ has given to his Church are the ordained ministries of bishops, priests, and deacons. These ministries have existed in the Church since New Testament times, although the concrete roles of each and their interrelationships have varied over the course of the Church's history. These three orders belong to the essence of the Church's ministry, and they are received by the Church as special ministries willed by Jesus Christ and empowered by a special grace of the Holy Spirit.

17.   The essential role of those in sacred orders is to lead the Church in carrying out the mission of Christ. The three ordained ministries coordinate all the other ministries and services by which the Church exists, lives, and acts. The role is, to apply the words of St. Paul, "to equip the saints [that is, the whole community] for the work of ministry, the building up of the Body of Christ."[19] Bishops, in a special way, preside over and govern the particular Churches, aided by the presbytery. The

18. See AA 2.
19. Eph 4:12.

11

role of the deacon is to be a helper of the bishops and priests and, graced by the sacrament, to proclaim by their very lives the Church's call to serve the needs of others.

B. THE MINISTRY OF THE DEACON

1. Identifying the Deacon

18. The diaconate had its origins in apostolic times and flourished in the first four centuries of the Church's history. Later, for very complex reasons, the diaconate went into decline. In the Eastern Church, the deacon's liturgical roles were fully retained, though the role of serving the needs of the community was gradually obscured. In the Western Church, the diaconate became little more than a step on the way to the priesthood.

19. It was the Second Vatican Council that restored the diaconate as a permanent ministry in the Church.[20] In the discussion before, and at the council that led to this decision, three primary motives were at work. The first was a desire to restore to the Church the full complement of active apostolic ministries. A second motive was the desire to integrate and strengthen with sacramental ordination and grace those who were, in fact, already exercising diaconal functions. The third goal was to provide ministers for those regions where functions vital to the Church's life could not be carried out.

20. Since the Catholic Church had not had any recent experience of the diaconate as an active ministry, it is not surprising that there has been some difficulty in articulating, both in theory and in practice, the distinctive nature and purpose of this ministry. The ancient practice of the diaconate has been of some assistance, but both the later developments of the episcopate and the priesthood and the great changes in the historical, ecclesiastical, and sociological circumstances of the Church since ancient days have made it impossible to take the early experience as an exact or adequate model for a contemporary diaconate. The diaconate has emerged in the postconciliar Church at the same time that lay ministries have flourished as seldom before and that some parts of the Church have experienced a grave decline in the number of priests. This has sometimes led

---

20. See LG 29.

to mistaken views, such as conceiving of the diaconate as a "lay ministry," regarding it as a threat to lay ministries, or seeing the deacon as a "mini-priest."

21. However, in the years since it was restored, the diaconate, especially in the United States, has developed in response to the pastoral needs of the Church. Deacons have been participating eagerly and creatively in the Church's pastoral activity, so that, in reflecting on the diaconate, we are able to draw upon Scripture, tradition, and a great deal of concrete experience. The portrait of the deacon that follows draws upon all these resources.

22. First of all, the diaconate is an ordained ministry. It belongs to those central ministries of leadership to which Jesus Christ has entrusted the fundamental task of assuring that the Church become and remain the authentic sacrament of salvation. In an ordination, a Christian blessed with the ability to minister is chosen from among the members of Christ to occupy an office and to fulfill a role representative of both Christ and the Church. In this sacrament, a bishop lays hands upon a man and, in the name of the Church, prays God to empower him with the gifts of the Spirit that will enable him to fulfill his particular role. The believing community then receives the man as one who, in his sacramental consecration, permanent commitment, and specific ministry, is a sacrament to it of Jesus Christ himself. Ordination is, thus, the sacramental differentiation of a Christian within the community of faith, so that he becomes for it a unique sign and instrument of what Jesus Christ is for the Church and of what the Church must be for the sake of Jesus Christ.

23. Second, the diaconate is a distinct order within the ordained ministry of the Church. The bishop, as successor to the apostles, presides over the local diocesan Church. To him is entrusted the primary responsibility of faithfully and integrally preaching the Word of God, of ministering the mysteries of God in the sacraments, and of governing the People of God. Within a diocese, priests assist the bishop as his representatives in and to the local communities of faith. They do so through the ministry of Word and sacrament and by guiding the communities in fidelity and charity.

24. In communion with the bishop and priests, deacons are ordained for a distinct ministry, which is indicated by their name: they are ordained, says the ancient tradition (repeated at

Vatican II), *for service*.[21] They function in all three areas of the Church's life: in the transmission of the Word, in the celebration of the sacraments, and in the community's active love.

25. To say, as the ancient tradition does, that deacons are ordained for *service* is to look to the needs of the Church and its members for the proper role of the diaconate. From the beginning, this has been the deacon's proper mark. Ancient descriptions of the deacon's task included a very broad range of specific charitable activities in which deacons are involved. This same orientation toward concrete service, especially of the most needy, neglected, and marginalized among Jesus Christ's brothers and sisters, has also been visible in many of the ministries undertaken by deacons since the diaconate was restored. Thus, concern for social ministry in the local Church is related to the long history of diaconal service.

26. It is not, of course, as if the deacon is the only one who engages in service in the Church. Service is a task that falls upon every Christian as an immediate duty of a life in obedience to and imitation of Christ; and service obviously is also a primary and central task of bishops and priests. But, the deacon especially has this role, in virtue of his ordination, to be a representative person in the Church. Pope Paul VI spoke of this active symbolic character when he described the deacon as "the animator and promoter [*instimulator*] of the Church's service or *diaconia* in local Christian communities, and as a sign or sacrament of the Lord Christ himself, who 'came not to be served but to serve.' "[22] The deacon, in other words, in his person and in his roles, continually makes visible to the Church the redemptive service fulfilled by Jesus Christ. At the same time, the deacon represents and promotes in the Church what the community of faith, as a whole and in all of its members, must be, namely, a community of service.

27. As it would be a distortion and betrayal of the ministries of bishops and priests to think that only they have responsibility for the upbuilding of the Church in faith or for the praise of God in worship, so also ordination to the diaconate does not set a man apart in order for him to have a monopoly on the

---

21. LG 29, quoting the *Constitutions of the Egyptian Church*, III, 2, and the *Statuta Ecclesiae Antiquae*, 37-41.
22. *Ad Pascendum*, Introduction.

Church's service. The deacon's distinctiveness is, rather, *sacramental:* what *all* in the Church are to be and to do is made visible and effective by the liturgical consecration and empowerment of *some* members among them. Within the one great sacrament of Jesus Christ which is the Church, the sacrament of orders symbolizes at once the unity and diversity of Christian service.

28. The deacon is also a representative symbol of the inner connections among the three great areas of the Church's life: Word, sacrament, and service. The ancient tradition appears to indicate that it was because the deacon was the servant at the table of the poor that he had his distinctive liturgical roles of gathering the gifts and distributing communion at the Table of the Lord. Similarly, there is a reciprocal correspondence between his role as a proclaimer of the Gospel and his role as an articulator of the needs of the Church in the general intercessions. In his formal liturgical roles, the deacon brings the poor to the Church and the Church to the poor. He thus symbolizes in his roles the grounding of the Church's life in the Eucharist and the mission of the Church in the loving service of the needy. In the deacon, in a unique way, is represented the relationship between the worship of God in the liturgy that recalls Jesus Christ's redemptive service and the worship of God in everyday life where Jesus Christ is again encountered in the needy.

29. It is, then, in the notion of a deacon as a sacramental symbol that his distinct identity is to be found. The tasks he performs, in any one area of his service, are ones that can be— and often are—performed by others in the community, and his ordination is not intended to remove those tasks from others. But, in the deacon these tasks are united in virtue of a sacramental ordination. In an ordination, the Church expresses in word and rite what it believes about the Christ whose disciple it claims to be, about the loving service to which that discipleship calls it as a whole, and about the inner link between Word, sacrament, and love; and, what the Church is saying sacramentally, the deacon represents in his person and in his ministry. The deacon is thus a sign and instrument of that manifold service without which the Church cannot be the sign and instrument of Jesus Christ.

2. The Call to the Diaconate

30. Deacons are ordained by the local bishop and for the service of the diocesan Church. It is this local Church that mediates God's call to the diaconal ministry. It is within this Church that a man has already demonstrated the gifts and ability to carry out this ministry. It is this Church that discerns and ratifies the call to ministry. It is this Church that, in the person of the bishop, prays God to bless the man and itself with the Spirit's gifts for ministry. It is to this Church that a deacon commits himself and is bound in service in communion with the bishop and priests.

31. Since it is defined by service, the diaconate is not an end in itself, nor is it to be used or sought as a way of honoring or rewarding a person. A man's personal inclination is also not itself a sufficient or even the primary consideration in the discernment of a diaconal vocation. This office, too, no one takes on himself. The local diocesan Church must always mediate the divine vocation through its choice and call.

32. Because the deacon's service is oriented to the whole of the local diocesan Church, the final judgment of a vocation rests with the bishop. To be ordained a deacon is to be committed to the broad range of a diocese's needs and concerns, to be ready to integrate one's own gifts and ministry into the larger pastoral commitments of the other ministers of the Church, and to be willing to exercise the diaconal ministry in obedience to the bishop's direction and in cooperation with the priests.

33. But, if the bishop has the final judgment, he is not the only one involved in the process of discerning a call to the diaconate. In those it would call to this ministry, the Church expects to find emotional maturity, personal integrity, Christian holiness, generosity for service, and a demonstration of the gifts needed for this ministry. These qualifications may be displayed most clearly and discerned most easily in smaller communities, such as the parishes where a man lives and works. It is here that the concrete needs of the Church and of others may first be experienced and recognized and that the abilities of a particular man to serve those needs may first be demonstrated and discerned. What the diaconate might concretely mean and who might be able and willing to carry it out are assessments that are really, though not exclusively, the responsibility of members of such communities. Reference to such communities must be made for an evaluation of a man who presents himself for the diaconate. It is quite appropriate and even desirable that such communities be encouraged to suggest to individuals that they

16

consider becoming deacons or to propose their names to those responsible for a diaconal program.

3. The Ministries of the Deacon

34. In the documents of Vatican II, and in the two decrees of Pope Paul VI that implemented the council's restoration of the diaconate, several lists of diaconal tasks are given.[23] These describe a broad range of activities deacons may perform. None of the lists is exhaustive, and some of the activities are left deliberately vague and open. In these documents, and as this ministry has developed in practice, it is possible to distinguish three general areas of diaconal ministry: love and justice, the Word, and liturgy. Something must now be said about each of these areas, about their integration, and about a ministry of leadership deacons may also be called upon to assume in particular circumstances.

a) The Ministry of Love and Justice

35. From its beginning, and particularly during the first centuries, the diaconate has been primarily a ministry of love and justice. The early metaphorical description of the deacon as "the eyes and ears, the mouth, heart, and soul of the bishop"[24] referred to the duty of the deacon to identify the needy, to report their needs to the bishop and the Church, and to direct the Church's loving service of them. Early descriptions of the duties of deacons place them among widows and orphans, with the sick and at the graves of the dead, and serving immigrants and exiles. In our own day, Pope Paul VI has spoken of the deacon as being "the interpreter of the needs and desires of Christian communities, the animator and promoter of the Church's service or *diaconia* in local Christian communities, and as a sign or sacrament of the Lord Christ himself, who 'came not to be served but to serve.' "[25]

36. As the diaconate has developed in the United States, a remarkably broad range of services to the needy has been assumed by deacons. In fact, it is hard to find a single category of needy

---

23. See LG 29 and AG 16, *Sacrum Diaconatus Ordinem*, V, 22, and *Ad Pascendum*, Introduction.
24. *Didascalia Apostolorum*, II, 44,4.
25. *Ad Pascendum*, Introduction.

people in Church and society who are not being served by deacons. The 1981 survey found deacons serving abused children, the aged, battered women, the bereaved, the blind, the deaf, the divorced, drug addicts, the dying, the handicapped, the homeless, the ill, prisoners, refugees, the rural poor, street people, victims of racial and ethnic discrimination, etc.[26] Deacons are meeting these people, in the name of the Church, and among them are representing the care of Jesus Christ the Servant. The ways in which these and other needy people are being helped vary greatly from place to place. It is a sign of the health of the diaconate in this country that so many new initiatives have been undertaken to bring Jesus Christ's healing and comforting Word and power to the physically, economically, and spiritually needy of our day.

37. Of course, deacons are not the only Christians involved in such care of the needy. Pope Paul VI spoke of deacons as animating and promoting the *common* service of the Church, and this is a task that needs emphasis. As by ordination, particularly and officially committed to service, the deacon is to inspire, promote and help coordinate the service that the whole Church must undertake in imitation of Christ. He has a special responsibility to identify *to* the Church those who are in need and particularly those who are without power or voice at the margins of our society. Among such people, the deacon is to speak about Christ and to offer them the Church's varied assistance. But *in* the Church, he is also to speak about the needy, to articulate their needs, and to inspire and mobilize the whole community's response. He thus becomes a representative figure in whom the Church reaches out to the needy and the needy challenge the Church.

38. This ministry of love is also a ministry of justice that aims not only at meeting immediate needs but also at addressing their structural and institutional causes. Action on behalf of social justice is thus an integral part of the deacon's ministry of love. He must not only assist the powerless and speak for the voiceless, but also help them to find their own voice and to assume power over their lives. This prophetic role of social criticism and reform can be carried out in specific ministries,

---

26. *A National Study of the Permanent Diaconate in the United States* (Washington, D.C.: USCC Office of Publishing and Promotion Services, 1981).

but deacons who have secular occupations also have many opportunities to carry it out in their everyday work.

b) The Ministry of the Word of God

39.　　The deacon's ministry of the Word is also a very far-ranging one. It may include proclaiming the Gospel at the liturgy, preaching, catechetical instruction and other forms of teaching, counseling, instruction of catechumens, giving retreats, outreach to alienated Catholics, parish renewal programs, etc. In the United States, deacons have become involved in all of these types of activities. Besides these more or less formal occasions, deacons may also have many opportunities to speak about Jesus Christ more informally, especially as they carry out their ministries of love and justice. Deacons who have secular occupations also are able to witness to the Gospel in the marketplace, where they meet the demands of their work both as committed Catholics and as ordained ministers and use the opportunities their work provides to bring the Gospel to bear on the concrete circumstances of everyday individual and social life. In turn, their secular involvement also can equip them to bring questions and insights to bear on the Gospel and can thus help lead the Church to a richer and deeper appreciation of the faith by which it lives.

40.　　According to the Code of Canon Law, ". . . deacons possess the faculty to preach everywhere, to be exercised with at least the presumed consent of the rector of the church, unless that faculty has been restricted or taken away by the competent ordinary or unless express permission is required by particular law."[27]

c) The Ministry of the Liturgy

41.　　The Second Vatican Council asserted that "the liturgy is the summit toward which the activity of the Church is directed and the source from which all its power flows."[28] This is as true of the deacon as it is of the Church in general. To the Church gathered in worship, the deacon both brings the gifts of the people and articulates their needs. At the eucharistic assembly,

---

27. CIC 764.
28. SC 10.

the deacon assists the community in its worship and helps to minister the great mystery of Jesus Christ's redemptive gift of himself in Word and sacrament. And, in such liturgical celebrations, in which all three of the deacon's ministries are uniquely concentrated and integrated, the deacon finds the source from which he draws his own Christian life and the grace to carry out his ministry.

42. At the Eucharist, the deacon may proclaim the Gospel, preach, voice the needs of the people in the general intercessions, assist in the presentation of the gifts, and distribute communion. The deacon can also perform other liturgical roles, such as solemnly baptizing, witnessing marriages, bringing Viaticum to the dying, and presiding over funerals and burials. In addition to these roles, he can also preside over liturgies of the Word, the Liturgy of the Hours, exposition and benediction of the Blessed Sacrament, lead nonsacramental reconciliation services, conduct prayer services for the sick and dying, and administer certain of the Church's sacramentals. The norm contained in the document *The Deacon, Minister of Word and Sacrament* serves as a useful reminder: In those instances where a deacon may wish to be a minister at a liturgical celebration in a parish or institution other than his own (e.g., marriage, baptism, funeral), he should first obtain the proper delegation.[29]

d) The Integration of the Diaconal Ministries

43. The diaconal ministries, distinguished above, are not to be separated; the deacon is ordained for them all, and no one should be ordained who is not prepared to undertake each in some way. This is not to say that a deacon may not have greater abilities in one ministry, and that, therefore, his ministry may not be marked by one of them more than by the others. But, there is an intrinsic relationship among the three areas of the deacon's ministry if he is to be a sign of the Servant-Christ who redeemed us as at once Prophet, Priest, and King. In his person and in his roles, the deacon is also to represent to the Church the full range of services which it itself is called to carry out in the world. When the deacon preaches or teaches, it is as one

---

29. For a full description of the liturgical ministries of the deacon, see *The Deacon, Minister of Word and Sacrament*, Bishops' Committee on the Liturgy, Study Text VI (Washington, D.C.: USCC Office of Publishing and Promotion Services, 1979), pp. 47-53.

whose ministry and presence in the world have well acquainted him with the needs of the people. When he ministers at the altar, he brings those needs to the Church and to Jesus Christ. As he ministers to the needy in his day-to-day service, so also at the Eucharist he ministers the Body of Christ to the People of God. And when he works for the needy, he does so as one who has himself both received and ministered the twofold bread of the Word and of the Eucharist.

e) Two Particular Leadership Roles

44.   According to Vatican II, Pope Paul VI's *Sacrum Diaconatus Ordinem*, and the *Code of Canon Law* (c. 517), deacons may also be given charge over the pastoral care of Christian communities that cannot be provided a pastor in the person of a priest. Full leadership over an integral local Christian community, of course, includes the ability to preside over the Eucharist and to reconcile sinners; and for this the deacon is not ordained. But in the absence of priests, the Church can invest a deacon with the authority to carry out and coordinate the other acts of pastoral care. While such ministry is not central to or typical of the diaconal ministry, and while it is not to be conceived of as being a "substitute priest," there are circumstances in which deacons may be entrusted with this responsibility.

45.   Besides such cases, deacons may also be involved in pastoral programs aimed at creating and guiding small Christian communities within parishes or in particular sectors of society. Many such communities unite integrally the spiritual and social justice dimensions of the Church. It is particularly appropriate, then, for a deacon to participate in such communities. Within them, he can be the animator and promoter of Christian community on a small scale or at the grass-roots level and can help to unite such groups together in the larger communities of the parish and diocese.

4. Varieties of Diaconal Ministry

46.   The restored diaconate can be undertaken and carried out in many different forms and ways. It can be assumed by married men, by celibates, or by those men in consecrated life. It can be exercised along with a secular occupation or as a deacon's principal or only responsibility. It can be quite general in scope or focused on particular concerns. It can be exercised by deacons working alone or in diaconal or other pastoral teams.

47.   Another and very important reason for diversity in the exercise of the diaconate is the variety of situations confronting local churches. Ordination is always the sacramental dedication of a particular person for a particular church, with its own strengths and weaknesses, needs and challenges. The diaconate is a service of the particular needs of local communities of faith. What the diaconal ministry ought to be in the concrete, therefore, will always be, to some degree, relative to the various types of communities in and for which deacons are ordained.

48.   In a country as large and as varied as the United States, therefore, it is not possible to give specific guidelines about the shape of the diaconate, as it will have to be exercised in various geographical areas and amid the ethnically, racially, economically, socially, and culturally diverse communities of today. The guidelines that follow are general national guidelines. It will be the task of dioceses, individually or as provinces, to make these guidelines more specific as may be required by the distinct character and needs of the particular churches in their varied situations.

Chapter II

Diocesan Diaconal Organization

A. THE OVERALL DIOCESAN PASTORAL PLAN

49.   The diaconal ministry is to be conceived and established as a response to the real needs of the local Church and its situation. These needs will vary from place to place, from time to time, and from culture to culture. What the diaconate can be and can do, then, cannot completely be delineated beforehand but only by a careful and discerning reading of the signs of the times, places, and cultures in which local churches exist.

50.   If the diaconate is to be, as Pope Paul VI described it, "the interpreter of the needs and desires of the Christian communities [and] the animator and promoter of the Church's service or *diaconia* in local Christian communities," then the diaconal ministry should be an integral part of an overall diocesan plan to meet the pastoral needs of the entire local Church. The diaconate will call forth an additional body of ministers who will be available for the service of the diocese. In turn, when the diaconate is conceived from the start as an integral part of an overall plan, deacons will have a richer and firmer sense of their own identity and purpose.

51.   A continuing catechesis should also accompany the establishment and development of the diaconal ministry. Such a catechesis should include a historical and theological explanation of the origins and distinctive nature of this ministry and of the reasons for which it has been restored to the Church. This catechesis can also be an opportunity for the bishop, priests, religious, and laity to discern the needs and challenges of the local Church, to consider the types of services needed in order to meet them, to tailor a diaconal program to address them, and to begin the process of considering which men in the church might be called upon to undertake the diaconal ministry.

B. STRUCTURES FOR DIACONAL FORMATION AND MINISTRY

52. The diocese should provide appropriate structures for the formation of candidates and to support the exercise of the diaconal ministry. Among such possible structures are an office responsible for formation, a policy board, admissions committee, evaluation committee, etc. These structures should be representative of the priests, deacons, religious, and laity and should reflect the variety of cultures and groups in the diocese. Those who are asked to fulfill these roles should be well informed about the diaconate and its implications for the diocese.

53. A director of the diaconate, who would also be head of the diaconal office, should be appointed by the diocesan bishop. The position may appropriately be filled by a deacon. Special care should be taken that there be continuity in this office.

54. The functions of the diaconal office include the following:

a. planning and supervising the formation program;
b. identifying and screening potential candidates and, if they are married, their wives;
c. evaluating performance of candidates;
d. proposing candidates to the bishop for ordination;
e. assisting in the preparation of the statement delineating the initial pastoral ministry of each deacon;
f. providing assistance for the continuing education and spiritual growth of deacons after ordination;
g. supporting deacons and their families;
h. encouraging and promoting diaconal community;
i. regular review of the formation program;
j. evaluating the diaconal ministry in the diocese.

55. In time, it may be advisable to separate the responsibility for postordination diaconal ministry from responsibility for formation, for example, by appointing a separate vicar for deacons.

56. Since the majority of deacons will retain their secular occupation and contribute their ministry freely to the Church, it is usual for the diocese to defray the costs of the screening and formation of candidates. Since ordination will establish a primary relationship with the diocese rather than a particular parish, generally it is unwise to expect that these expenses be sustained solely by the candidate's parish of origin or by the parish where he will minister.

57.   According to *Sacrum Diaconatus Ordinem*,[1] deacons are to be represented on pastoral councils. Indeed, deacons should be included on all appropriate levels of pastoral consultation. Further, the diocesan bishop may fittingly establish a representative body of deacons to consult on matters affecting the diaconate, to give visible expression to their essential unity with him in the service of the Church.

C. APPROVAL AND EVALUATION OF DIOCESAN DIACONAL PROGRAMS

58.   When a diaconal program is introduced or substantially modified, the bishop must submit a detailed proposal to the Bishops' Committee on the Permanent Diaconate for approval. By this process, the National Conference of Catholic Bishops fulfills the requirements of *Ad Pascendum*.[2] This proposal should provide information on the following elements of the diaconal program:

    a. catechesis of priests, religious, and laity;
    b. recruitment of candidates and effective screening of candidates and wives of married candidates;
    c. the theological curriculum and methodology;
    d. the spiritual formation;
    e. the pastoral formation;
    f. the quality of the faculty;
    g. integration into the program of wives and families of married candidates;
    h. adaptation of the program to the ethnic and cultural characteristics of the diocese;
    i. evaluation of the candidates and of the program itself;
    j. provisions for the formation of diaconal community;
    k. procedures for the assignment of deacons;

---

1. *Sacrum Diaconatus Ordinem*, V, 24.
2. *Ad Pascendum*, VII, b.

l. provisions for both ministry and life after ordination, including continuing education, spiritual growth, and growth in diaconal community;

m. provision for the establishment of appropriate structures for the integration of deacons and the diaconal community among other diocesan structures.

59. Formal evaluation of a local program by a visiting team organized by the Bishops' Committee on the Permanent Diaconate and under the chairmanship of one of its members is available by application to the Bishops' Committee. This evaluation may be considered after a program has been functioning for at least three years.

Chapter III

The Formation of Deacons

A. THE SELECTION OF CANDIDATES

1. Identifying the Candidates

60. As indicated above, the introduction and development of the diaconate should always include a thorough catechesis both of the clergy and laity, indicating the nature of the diaconate, the types of service it entails, the way in which it fits into the overall diocesan pastoral plan, and the qualifications required in candidates. The more widespread and complete such instruction is, the more likely it is that prospective candidates will be attracted to this ministry.

61. The call to ordained ministry comes from God through the Church, which has the responsibility to determine if a vocation is truly present. In this country and elsewhere, the majority of deacons have taken the initiative in presenting themselves as candidates. In these cases, an initial attraction or desire is later submitted to the evaluation by which the Church, in the person of the bishop, finally determines whether a person has a genuine vocation.

62. It also may happen—and, in fact, should be encouraged—that local communities, in fulfilling their responsibility for the life of their churches, consider what the needs of their communities are and who there might be among their members who could effectively exercise a diaconal ministry in response to those needs.

63. Finally, as part of a coherent pastoral plan in which deacons will have an important role, dioceses or parishes may engage in active recruitment for the diaconate. A program of this sort will seek to identify potential candidates, describe the challenges and opportunities of the diaconal ministry to them, and urge them to consider it as a service to which they can commit themselves.

64. In the last two cases, the initiative in a call to the diaconate comes from the community. While obviously no one should be constrained to seek this ministry, such an invitation may be a providential way in which a man first considers seriously the possibility that God may be calling him to the diaconate. Such an initiative is not itself a vocation in the strict sense, which is only considered to be present when a bishop calls a man to orders.

65. In all these cases, the essential principle is that the diaconate is a *ministry*, a way of serving the Church, and never merely an honor or personal reward. The identity and ministry of the deacon are the primary criteria for deciding whether to admit a person to candidacy. Important general criteria include an integral Christian faith, personal integrity, maturity, holiness, regular participation in the Church's sacramental life, and evidence of previous, respected commitment to the Church's life and service and, for married candidates, a stable family life. More particular criteria will vary in accordance with the specific needs of the local diocesan Church and the general lines of its pastoral program.[1] It is the responsibility of the director and/or the diaconal board, under the bishop, to draw up these criteria, to review them regularly, and to evaluate prospective candidates in their light.

2. The Application and Acceptance of Candidates

66. The procedures for formal application and acceptance may differ in minor, specific details, but will be fundamentally alike in all diocesan programs.

---

1. For example, so long as the potential candidate is intelligent and articulate, the levels of education required will vary in accordance with different community needs and expectations and with the different types of ministry envisaged for a particular community or for a particular deacon.

a) Certain documents (or equivalents) are expected:
   (1) certificates of baptism, confirmation and, where relevant, marriage;
   (2) health evaluation;
   (3) written statement of consent from the wife of the candidate;
   (4) letter of recommendation from the pastor or other priest and, where possible, the parish council;
   (5) letters of recommendation from colleagues and, if possible, employers.
b) In accord with Canon Law,[2] the National Conference of Catholic Bishops has established the minimum age of ordination at thirty-five years for both married and celibate candidates. The diocesan bishop may dispense up to one year from this age requirement.[3]
c) To determine motivation and suitability, a process of screening that includes documentation, interviews, and the use of professional, psychological screening instruments for both the candidate and, if married, his wife is a critical element in the acceptance procedure. Written screening procedures scored by a psychologist are considered to be standard, but a psychologist and/or a psychiatrist may also be part of an interview team.

67. The admissions committee is responsible for advising the director of formation in the selection of candidates. It should review the documents, forms, reports of interviews, and the results of the professional screening procedures in reaching a judgment on the acceptance of applicants. This judgment is equivalent to a recommendation to the diocesan bishop, concerning the acceptability of each application. Members of the admissions committee may often be involved in the interviewing of potential candidates, either as a team, visiting the home of the applicant, or as a body, interviewing the applicants and, if married, the wives of the applicants as well.

---

2. See CIC 1031:3.
3. See CIC 1031:4.

B. THE FORMATION PROGRAM

1. General Remarks

68. The most important characteristics of a diaconal formation program are that it be (1) primarily pastoral in orientation, (2) theologically sound and well integrated, and (3) adapted to local resources and needs.

69. Deacons are ordained for service, to fulfill an important role in the upbuilding and activity of the local Church. Just as demonstrated ability to carry out such service is the primary criterion for admission to candidacy, so the needs of the Church and the diaconal ministries envisaged as a response to them must direct the preparation of men for this ministry.

70. For the same reason, the formation program must be well integrated. While the theological, pastoral, and spiritual dimensions of the program will be distinguished below, they are not utterly separable departments. No pastoral practice is likely to be effective if it does not at once derive from sound theological preparation and promote continued theological reflection. Nor is one likely to be a good deacon in Christ's Church if he does not himself live a committed Christian life, with a specifically diaconal spirituality of service. Therefore, the theological, pastoral, and spiritual dimensions of the formation program must be so interrelated that they promote a living integration in the exercise of diaconal ministry.

71. These formation guidelines are deliberately general in nature and need to be adapted in accordance with the geographical, social, economic, and cultural circumstances of the local Church, with its varying resources and needs, and with the general and specific character of diocesan pastoral programs and ministerial goals.

72. The wives and families of married candidates should be involved in the various aspects of the formation program. Relationships among deacons and their wives and children are bound to be affected by the new commitments that deacons make. These changes will be handled much more easily if the wives and at least the older children gain an understanding and appreciation of the new ministry that their husbands and fathers will be undertaking and of how it will affect them. Diaconal commitments and family relationships will thus enrich and confirm one another.

73.   According to the Code of Canon Law,[4] the formation program must last at least three years. Depending on the geography and culture of the local diocesan Church, and on the availability of staff and resources, the formation program may be structured on one of several models. The most common models of a program are weekly night-school sessions or monthly weekend meetings. The night-school model meets for an average of at least three hours per week and gathers candidates for periodic weekends throughout the academic year. Weekend sessions or programs can offer valuable occasions for different types of group dynamics and for building community among the candidates and their wives and children.

74.   Where geographical factors are particularly difficult and demanding, as in the dioceses of several western states, Alaska, Hawaii, and the island territories, still another model is utilized. This may require that the number of years in formation be extended or that the length of sessions be increased. Creative uses of modern technological communication or travelling formation teams should be considered to meet the special requirements of such areas.

2. Theological Formation

75.   Several general criteria should govern the theological formation of deacons. First, as already noted, the program is designed to prepare candidates to exercise a pastoral ministry. The theological program should therefore be oriented toward ministry, providing the candidate with the knowledge and appreciation of the faith that he needs in order to be able to carry out his ministry of Word, sacrament, and service. It should also promote the deacon's lifelong effort to reflect on his ministry in the light of faith. Theology should thus be presented as originating in the Church's life of faith, worship, and love and as something crucial to the deacon's responsible exercise of his ministry.

76.   Second, theological formation should take into account the general needs of diaconal service in the communities for

---

4. CIC 236.

31

which a man is to be ordained. It should also be constructed in such a way that a candidate is helped to evaluate his society and culture in light of the Gospel and to understand the Gospel in light of the particular features of the society and culture in which he will be serving. This permits and requires a certain amount of latitude in the construction of theological programs and in the evaluation of candidates' performances.

77.   Third, since candidates enter the program as mature men, and since the majority of them are married and engaged in secular occupations, the theological formation should make use of the methods and processes of adult education. Candidates should be invited to draw and reflect upon their adult life and faith experiences. This should be taken into account in determining the types of courses to be offered and the types of educational experiences to be made available.

78.   An increasingly educated society demands that deacons be knowledgeable and reliable witnesses of the faith and spokesmen for the Church's teaching. The theological program, therefore, should be designed to communicate such a knowledge of the faith and church traditions that they will be able to carry out this vital ministry. Candidates should be expected to be familiar with the teaching of the Second Vatican Council and with more recent official church teaching. The program should include the following subjects:

a. an introduction to the Scriptures and to critical interpretation of the Bible: a theology of the Old Testament; the New Testament, especially the Gospels and Epistles; the relationship between Scripture and tradition; how to use the Scriptures in preaching, catechesis, counseling, etc.;
b. fundamental theology: the sources, themes, and methods of theology; revelation, faith, and reason;
c. the faith of the Church: the mystery of God the Creator and Redeemer; Christology; ecclesiology; the role of the Blessed Virgin Mary; Christian anthropology; sacraments and liturgy, especially the theology of ministry;
d. Christian morality in both its personal and social dimensions;
e. the canon law of the Church;
f. the history of the Church.

79. The initial program, and any substantial revisions of it, should spell out in detail how these theological requirements are to be met; it should then be submitted to the Bishops' Committee on the Permanent Diaconate for review and approval.

80. To assist the theological reflection, which should be a permanent element of the service deacons perform, the theological program should encourage and guide candidates in building up a personal library of theological resources that will be useful to them later.

81. Candidates are to be held accountable for their performance in their theological formation. How this is to be accomplished is left up to the judgment of those responsible for the diaconal formation program.

3. Pastoral Formation

82. The entire formation program should have a pastoral focus. Its immediate concern is to provide the necessary knowledge, sensitivities, and skills for those who will be dedicated to a special ministry of service in the community, and who will be officially and publicly recognized for this by the Church, through ordination. The program should take into account the fact that candidates preparing for the diaconate have already been involved in the mission of the Church, where they have demonstrated the natural and spiritual gifts that make them likely candidates. It should be designed in such a way as to build upon previous experience and talents already displayed. The academic, spiritual, and pastoral formation faculty should be equally sensitive to and actively involved in the effort to bring about fresh, creative responses to the gospel message in the various cultural and ethnic situations arising in the local Church.

83. In addition to identifying, improving, and furthering the gifts already at work, the program should aim at helping the candidate to discover talents, perhaps unrecognized, and to develop the skills necessary for this new ministry. At the end of the program, the candidates should have both a genuine confidence in their abilities and a realistic sense of their own limitations.

84. During formation, engagement in a wide diversity of pastoral services, at least on a limited basis, will not only give the candidate a greater awareness of the needs and mission of the local Church, but will assist in the discernment and development of his own particular personal talents and gifts. It should provide an opportunity for theological reflection as well as occasions to translate theory into practice, as his talents are increasingly identified. Competent, objective, and sympathetic supervision will be required. While the talents of the deacon must always be taken into account, he should be made aware as part of his spiritual formation that the needs of the Church remain central in his future ministry.

85.   Supervision is a specialized skill, not simply a combination of age and good will. The diocese must be committed to the preparation of skillful ministerial supervisors who possess pastoral experience, knowledge of the art of supervision, and a keen awareness that they are assisting mature men with life experiences of their own. In some instances, professional supervisory personnel will already be present in social welfare agencies, hospitals, and prisons. In other instances, the same level of proficiency may not be available, and competent supervisors will need to be trained.

86.   In addition to the theological courses offered, certain other courses more immediately directed to skillful pastoral practice should be offered in the academic curriculum. Among them are the following:
   a. Liturgical practice: the meaning of liturgy and symbol; the proper administration of liturgical rites and devotions; the sacraments and sacramentals; proper and effective proclamation of the Word; and the deacon's role in assisting at the eucharistic liturgy.[5]
   b. A process for discerning the charisms and skills for homiletic proclamation of the Word. Although every deacon will proclaim the Word in a variety of situations, the public proclamation of the Word in homilies at Mass, in the administration of the sacraments, and in other liturgical rites is a particular and sacred skill. There should be practical exercises on effective preaching.
   c. Courses on the principles of Christian social justice and their implementation; parish social ministry; skills in providing direct assistance to the needy in a respectful manner.

---

5. See *The Deacon, Minister of Word and Sacrament*, Study Text VI (Washington, D.C.: USCC Office of Publishing and Promotion Services, 1979).

d. An introduction to psychology, with particular attention to methods of counseling individuals and groups; recognition of the need for referral for professional attention.
   e. Courses in sociology, community organization, etc., with particular attention to applications in the local pastoral situation.
   f. When it is anticipated that deacons will participate in the pastoral care of parishes or communities,[6] the program should provide training in the necessary canonical, administrative, and pastoral skills.

87. The candidate should be made familiar with social service agencies, such as Catholic Charities and Family Life Bureaus, as a point of referral and a source of training, as well as a potential field for active ministry.

88. The demonstration of pastoral skills by the candidate is a crucial element in the evaluation of his fitness for ordination. Those responsible for the formation program are to determine how the evaluation of pastoral skills is to be carried out.

89. The program for pastoral formation should be detailed in the proposal submitted to the Bishops' Committee on the Permanent Diaconate for approval.

4. Spiritual Formation

90. While the spiritual program is here being described as a separate dimension of the formation of deacons, it should be conceived and designed as the element that integrates the other two dimensions. The deacon should be prepared in such a way that his life as the Church's minister forms an integrated whole of professional skills and personal commitment and devotion to Christ and the Church.

91. As with all other Christians, the deacon's spiritual life, founded on his baptism, should be centered in the Paschal Mystery of Christ. His faith should be constantly nourished by reading and meditating on the Scriptures. His activity should be enlivened and strengthened by regular participation in the sacraments, especially the Eucharist and the sacrament of rec-

---

6. See CIC 517; also see *Sacrum Diaconatus Ordinem*, V, 10.

onciliation. And his personal Christian life should have a strong ecclesial and communal dimension.

92.   Since he is an ordained minister, the deacon's spiritual life should have a powerful ministerial dimension. He does not go before God simply as an individual Christian, but also as a deacon whose consecration and commitment bring unique responsibilities, challenges, and opportunities. With him when he prays to God, must also come those with whom and for whom he serves in the Church. The spiritual challenges and responsibilities common to the Christian are in the deacon focused and qualified by his ministerial challenges and responsibilities.

93.   The program of spiritual formation should build upon the candidates' previous adult Christian experience and commitments, especially, in the case of married deacons, their commitment to wife and family. A man should not be admitted to the program who has not demonstrated the personal integrity and maturity and the Christian commitment and generosity that make him a likely candidate for the diaconal ministry. The spiritual program should be able to presume his Christian adulthood and seriousness. The varying quality and depth of these qualities should be taken into account in helping candidates grow in self-knowledge, in their commitment to Christ and his Church, and in their dedication to service.

94.   One of the chief aims of the spiritual program should be to assist the candidate in achieving a spiritual integration of his life and ministry. Most candidates are married men who also have secular occupations. The ministry they undertake has to be carried out in a way that draws upon the riches of their family life and respects their duties at home and at work, and for this, they need a spiritual life in which ministry, family, and occupation enrich and confirm one another. For this reason, the wives of candidates should be closely involved in the activities for spiritual formation. This common participation in the program will often strengthen and enrich their marriages.

95.   The goals of the spiritual formation program are many:

    a. to assist the candidate, with the help of his spiritual director and those responsible for the program, in discerning whether or not he has a vocation to the diaconate;

    b. to deepen and cultivate his commitment to Christ and the Church;

c. to help him integrate his new ministerial commitment with his previous commitments to family and to work;

d. to strengthen the personal and ministerial charisms he has already demonstrated in his life;

e. to develop the personal qualities and abilities that will be needed in his ministry;

f. to help him grow in self-knowlege and to develop the habit of repentance and self-criticism in light of the Gospel and of his ministerial responsibilities;

g. to deepen his prayer-life: personal, familial, communal, and liturgical;

h. to acquaint him with the Catholic spiritual tradition, especially as reflected in classic spiritual writings and in the examples of the saints, and with contemporary developments in spirituality;

i. to prepare him for the challenges of spiritual leadership that his ministry will entail.

96. The spiritual program should offer candidates a variety of prayer and retreat experiences. These will be helpful, not only in giving them opportunities to test the various traditional and contemporary approaches to the spiritual life, but also in enriching the spiritual ministry they will be able to offer people in their ministry.

97. Candidates should be introduced to and encouraged to pray the Liturgy of the Hours, since it is the official prayer of the Church and gives a firm liturgical direction to their prayer. Deacons should be expected to know the nature and structure of the Liturgy of the Hours and be able to lead it publicly. Although they are not bound by the universal church law to say the whole of this prayer every day, permanent deacons should not hold themselves lightly excused from the obligation they have to recite morning and evening prayer.[7]

98. At their ordination, deacons make a lifelong promise of obedience to their diocesan bishop. The formation program should explore with the candidates the nature and extent of this obligation and its implications for their ministry, their marriage, and their personal spiritual life.

---

7. See canon 276:3. The wording of this sentence was adopted by the NCCB Administrative Committee on September 11, 1985.

99.   The spiritual formation program should also aim at equipping and motivating candidates to continue their spiritual growth after ordination. During their formation, they should be encouraged to secure the assistance of a personal spiritual advisor, to cultivate regular patterns of prayer and sacramental participation, and to take the time to reflect spiritually on their ministry. It will be useful if, even during the period of formation, they form and take part in diaconal communities, groups in which they will be able to reflect together on the challenges and opportunities of their ministries.

100.   Unmarried men, upon ordination, make a lifetime commitment to celibacy. Special provisions should be made in the spiritual formation program to prepare them for the celibate life. They should be instructed in the meaning and value of celibacy, helped to make such a serious commitment, given concrete and useful advice on dealing with its difficulties and problems, and encouraged to develop the spiritual and communal resources necessary to live it faithfully.

101.   The proposals submitted to the Bishops' Committee on the Permanent Diaconate should spell out in detail how the program of spiritual formation is to be carried out.

5. Evaluation and Ordination

102.   Regular evaluations of candidates should be made and communicated to them and to the diocesan bishop each year during the formation program. These should review the candidate's performance in all areas of the program. If conducted seriously and communicated frankly, such reviews can be valuable occasions for the candidate's development and for the discernment of a vocation. These evaluations should be carried out by all those responsible for the formation program, supervised by the diocesan diaconal committee, and submitted to the bishop by the director of the diaconate.

103.   At the completion of the formation period, a final evaluation of the candidate's suitability for ordination must be made to the bishop. It must testify to the candidate's faith and theological development, his moral and spiritual maturity, his fidelity to marriage (or celibacy), and his ability to minister. This evaluation is equivalent to a recommendation that the bishop call the candidate to the order of deacon.

104. Before a candidate can be ordained, the following documents must be submitted:

    a. a declaration that the course of studies has been completed;[8]

    b. baptismal, confirmation, and, for married candidates, marriage certificates;[9]

    c. a declaration that the ministries of lector and acolyte have been received and exercised, that interstices have been observed, and that a profession of faith has been made and signed;[10]

    d. a handwritten declaration by the candidate of his free and lifelong commitment to the ecclesiastical ministry, and of his petition to receive the order of deacon;[11]

    e. a written statement of consent from the wife of a married candidate.[12]

105. All other canonical requirements, possible irregularities, and impediments must be considered,[13] unless legitimately modified or dispensed by law or competent authority (e.g., period of probation, age, rite of celibacy for unmarried candidates, liturgical rite of candidacy, health, retreat, irregularities),[14] as well as other requirements, such as dimissorial letters, which may apply in particular cases.[15]

---

8. CIC 1027; 1032:3; 1050:1; 1051:1.
9. CIC 1050:3.
10. CIC 1035; 833:6.
11. CIC 1036.
12. CIC 1050:3.
13. CIC 1024-1054.
14. CIC 1040-1049.
15. CIC 1050-1052.

Chapter IV

Married Deacons

106. For centuries, the Latin Church has had the experience of only celibate ordained ministers. Experience of ordained ministers who are married is recent. Special attention, catechesis, and direction must be given to this aspect of ministry, particularly to the mutual relationship between the sacrament of marriage and the sacrament of orders. Self-giving love is common to both sacraments. During this formation, as well as after ordination, the candidates and their wives need to appreciate this potential for an integrated spirituality that relates the two sacraments.

107. A stable marriage and loving family life are positive attributes contributing to this new ministry. In describing the family as the domestic Church,[1] the Second Vatican Council notes that parents are the "first heralds of the faith to their children"; significantly, the same word is employed in the ceremony of ordination when the deacon is told, "receive the Gospel of Christ whose herald you are. . . ." This mandate and this familial relationship should be evident and efficacious in both the formation and ministry of married deacons. The married deacon must never lose sight of a practical order of priorities: the sacrament of matrimony preceded the sacrament of orders and thus established a practical priority in the deacon's life. Consequently, he must be able to support his wife and family before he can be acceptable as an ordained minister. The marriage bond should be enriched by the sacrament of orders,

---

1. LG 11.

just as public ministry is enriched by married ordained ministers of the Gospel.

108.   The revised Code of Canon Law requires the written consent of the wife to her husband's ordination.[2] The consent should be an informed consent. For this reason, it is strongly recommended that the wife of the candidate participate as fully as possible in the entire program of formation, including taking courses, social gatherings, and retreats. A 1981 national study[3] demonstrated that wives who participated most fully in the formation and ministry of their husbands manifested the highest degree of satisfaction and the lowest degree of stress. The truly informed consent of the wife also means that she should have the benefit of the same extent of psychological screening as her candidate husband.

109.   There should be opportunities during the course of formation for the wives of candidates to discuss and share their insights, apprehensions, and concerns. These exchanges are most properly coordinated by the wife or a committee of wives of diaconal candidates or ordained deacons, even though a professional may assist in the direction of formal sessions.

110.   Even though it is clearly understood from the outset that the wife is not to be ordained, nevertheless her marriage and family are truly involved. The deacon and his wife will need to make a realistic assessment of how her own career, ministry, family, and personal preference will be affected and respected. They have to be aware that the nurturing and deepening of their mutual sacrificial love will be the most important way that she will be involved in her husband's public ministry in the Church. Good spiritual direction can help both the wife and husband in understanding and appreciating this truth.

111.   The wife of the deacon may become involved in a type of team ministry with her deacon husband. On the other hand, she may already be involved in a distinct ministry apart from the diaconal ministry of her husband. Having experienced the formation process of her husband, she may now wish to consider a type of ministry she had not foreseen but for which she is now significantly qualified. The local Church should recog-

---

2. See CIC 1050:3.
3. *A National Study of the Permanent Diaconate in the United States* (Washington, D.C.: USCC Office of Publishing and Promotion Services, 1981).

nize the rich ministerial potential that may be present in the wives of ordained deacons who have participated in the full formation process, and should they choose to offer themselves in ministry, facilitate the utilization of this potential.

112. Insofar as possible, depending upon their ages, the children should be informed and involved in the formation of their candidate father. This should be to the extent that they are interested and appreciate to what degree their lives will be affected by his ordination. Programs, particularly of a social-spiritual nature, can be developed to assist the children in maintaining healthy, unaffected relationships with their peers.

113. The Code of Canon Law preserves the traditional discipline of the Church, whereby a married deacon who has been widowed may not enter a new marriage.[4] The bishop and diaconal community will surely provide consolation, understanding, and direction through this painful adjustment. Dispensation from the law can be granted only by the Holy See. It is important that the implications of the Church's law in this regard be realisticly addressed during the period of formation. Widows of permanent deacons should be given similar sympathetic understanding by the local Church.

---

4. CIC 1087.

42

Chapter V

Ministry and Life after Ordination

114.   At ordination, a deacon enters into new sets of relationships that define his position in the Church. This chapter will briefly review the deacon's relationships with his bishop, with priests, with his fellow deacons, and with the laity.

A. RELATIONSHIPS WITH THE BISHOP AND DIOCESAN CHURCH

115.   A deacon is ordained for the service of a diocesan Church. Ordained by its bishop, the deacon stands in a direct relationship with his diocesan bishop, in communion with whom and under whose authority he exercises his ministry. By virtue of his ordination, a deacon is canonically incardinated into a specific diocese.

116.   It is the bishop who assigns a deacon to a particular ministry. The principal criteria for this assignment are the pastoral needs of the diocese and of local communities and the personal qualifications and abilities of the deacon, as these have been discerned in his previous experience and the course of his formation. The assignment should also take into account his family and occupational responsibilities.

117.   It is very important that the particular ministry assigned to a deacon by his bishop be very clearly spelled out, preferably in a written document of mission. It should always contain a clear delineation of responsibilities, that is, of the expectations of the diocese, of the particular community in and for which the deacon serves, and of the deacon himself. Such job descriptions will go far to prevent misunderstandings and disappointments arising among either the deacons themselves or other members of the Church. This mission should be regularly evaluated and reviewed and may be revised when changes in church needs or in the development of the deacon himself suggest it.

118. The bishop is also responsible for supervising the ministerial life of deacons. He should, therefore, encourage and support them in their work, involve them in the committees and councils that assist him in the pastoral care of the diocese, promote their spiritual lives by providing spiritual counselors and opportunities for prayer and reflection, and provide continuing education programs for them.

119. Married deacons who devote themselves completely to the ecclesiastical ministry deserve a remuneration by which they can provide for their own support and that of their families. Married deacons, however, who receive remuneration by reason of a civil profession that they exercise or have exercised are to take care of their own and their family's needs from the incomes derived from their profession.[1] Expenses incurred by deacons in the exercise of their ministry should be recompensed by the agency, institution, parish, or diocese for which the ministry is undertaken.

120. Should a deacon, after his ordination, move to another diocese, the procedures for excardination and incardination are the same as those for priests.[2] A deacon who moves from one diocese to another will ordinarily be admitted by the bishop into the diaconal ministry of his new diocese, at least after a period of time sufficient for the new diocese to become acquainted with the deacon and for him to become acquainted with the new diocese and with the order of deacons already at work there. If the new diocese has not implemented the diaconate, the deacon will not exercise his ministry without the permission of the bishop.

---

1. CIC 281:3.
2. See CIC 267-272.

B. RELATIONSHIPS WITH PRIESTS

121. Deacons exercise their distinct ministry in communion not only with the bishop but also with priests. The priesthood and the diaconate are neither identical nor competitive, but, rather, complementary ministries. The diaconate is not an abridged form of the priesthood, but a distinct and full order in its own right. Both priests and deacons should understand, then, that the diaconate is not to be thought of or exercised on the model of the priesthood. Deacons and priests should have a genuine respect for each other and for the integrity of the two distinct ministries. For the good of the Church, the two ministries must be exercised in communion with one another.

122. A catechesis of the presbyterate should be part of the introduction and development of the diaconate in a diocese. In it, priests will be informed of the nature and functions of deacons, encouraged to collaborate in a fuller diocesan pastoral program of which deacons will be an integral part, and urged both to make the new ministry known to their people and to seek out suitable candidates for this ministry. If difficulties or tensions arise between priests and deacons, the bishop should take steps to resolve the problems for the sake of the common good of the Church.

123. As in a diocese, so also in a parish, other type of community, institution, or agency, the introduction of deacons should be part of an overall pastoral plan. If a deacon is likely to be assigned to a parish, the priests and people there should be involved in drawing up the formal document of diaconal mission (see 116, above). In this way, priests, deacons, and people will all have a clear vision of what may be expected from the new ministers; the work of the local community will be facilitated; and tensions will be much less likely. Serious consideration should be given to deacons being members of pastoral teams and participating in parish councils.

C. COMMUNITY AMONG DEACONS

124. It is part of the meaning of ordination that a man is, by this sacrament, brought into the *ordo* or body of ordained ministers. A communal element is thus essential to ordination and to the exercise of ordained ministry. The mutual support and fraternity of deacons are not just sociologically or psychologically useful things; they are integral parts of the meaning of their vocation.

125. Deacons are, therefore, encouraged to cultivate a sense of community among themselves. They have a diaconal ministry toward one another, too, which they can exercise in countless ways, both informally and formally, as, for example, by establishing regional or diocesan diaconal communities. In these communities, they can meet regularly to pray and to reflect together about their work, to address common problems, to study together, and to support one another. Contacts and meetings, both formal and informal, are encouraged on a national level also, so that the greatly varying experiences of the diaconate throughout the country may be both a challenge and a support.

126. As the diaconal ministry matures in a diocese, it is only natural that deacons be brought into the process of planning, directing, and evaluating the program. Candidates for the diaconate will be helped and encouraged if qualified deacons are found among their directors and teachers.

127. According to *Sacrum Diaconatus Ordinem*,[3] deacons are, as far as possible, to take part in pastoral councils.

D. RELATIONSHIPS WITH THE LAITY

128. By virtue of their ordination, deacons become members of the clergy, with the rights and responsibilities that follow from that position. They are a unique instance of the clergy, however, since most of them are married, have secular occupations,[4] and do not engage in the Church's ministry as their sole activity. This combination of an ordained ministry with marriage and secular occupation can be a great strength to their ministry and a great opportunity for the Church as a whole. Deacons are, thus, unusually qualified to represent the presence of the Church to the world and the needs and challenges of the world to the Church.

---

3. *Sacrum Diaconatus Ordinem*, V, 24.
4. CIC 288.

129. Deacons should consider it an important part of their ministry of service to promote and inspire that participation in the life and activity of the Church, which the laity have as a right and duty by virtue of their baptism, confirmation, and charisms. The diaconate must never be seen or experienced as competitive or threatening to the lay apostolate or to lay ministries. The same Second Vatican Council that restored the diaconate as a permanent ministry also gave new impetus to lay involvement; and it would be a betrayal of the council's fundamental vision of the Church if one of these initiatives should be considered to impede the other. The whole Church is a communion of ministries and services, and the deacon is in a unique position to foster and to integrate the variety of activities that this communion requires.

130. The Code of Canon Law exempts permanent deacons from the obligation of wearing ecclesiastical garb.[5] However, in exceptional circumstances, a diocesan bishop, with due consideration for the practice of neighboring dioceses and with appropriate consultation, may decide that deacons should wear some distinctive garb when engaged in formal clerical ministry. For liturgical services, of course, the rubrical vesture is required. The bishop, likewise, is to determine what title or titles (if any) may be used to indicate diaconal status and the circumstances in which these may be used.

131. While the Code of Canon Law permits permanent deacons to hold political office,[6] a deacon should consult with his bishop before seeking or accepting such an office. In particular cases, the bishop may forbid such an undertaking.

132. Although most deacons will give only part of their time to formal diaconal ministries, they should not neglect the opportunities they have to exercise their ministry in the world or in the marketplace. They do not cease to be deacons when they go to their secular occupations, and there is much that they can do there precisely as deacons. Of course, a deacon should never use his ministry for the purposes of professional or personal gain. The diaconate is a ministry through which the needs of the world are brought to the Church, and the gifts the Church has to offer are brought to the world. This mediating role can

---

5. Ibid.
6. Ibid.

47

be made visible in particularly powerful ways by the manner in which the deacon fulfills his secular occupation and his civic and public responsibilities. In turn, deacons should be able to bring to the Church the appreciation of the meaning and value of the Gospel that derives from their regular and deep involvement in the world, bearing as they do both the questions the world has to pose and the unique insights secular activity can provide.

Conclusion

133.   The diaconate was restored as a permanent ministry both out of a concern to regain for the Church the full range of its ordained ministers and to meet the challenges of a new age. These guidelines have been drawn up on the basis of the Church's tradition, the challenges of Christian service in modern society, and in light of the experience gained in the years since the diaconate was restored in this country. It is the hope of the Bishops' Committee on the Permanent Diaconate that, as adapted in accordance with local resources and needs, they will prove to be of assistance to all those who share the burden and the privilege of representing the Servant Christ to the Servant Church.

Deacons in Institutes of Consecrated Life*

134. In his Motu Proprio of June 18, 1967, *Sacrum Diaconatus Ordinem*, Pope Paul VI reserved to the Holy See the right to institute, examine, and approve the recommendations of the general chapters of religious communities concerning the establishment of the permanent diaconate in such communities (VII, 32): "The institution of the permanent diaconate among the religious is a right reserved to the Holy See which is exclusively competent to examine and approve the recommendations of the general chapters in the matter."

135. The general norms for the restoration of the permanent diaconate also stipulate that the exercise of this ministry be under the authority of the bishop and the religious superior (VII, 33). There may be no exercise of this ministry in areas lacking a permanent diaconate, except with the consent of the local ordinary (VII, 34). Religious are bound by the laws to which members of the same religious family are obliged (VII, 33), and norms in force for religious priests will affect religious permanent deacons as well (VII, 33). Finally, it is stated that these provisions likewise apply to members of other institutes who profess the evangelical counsels (VII, 35).

---

*Approved by the Bishops' Committee on the Permanent Diaconate and the Conference of Major Superiors of Men in 1976 and 1983.

136. For these reasons, the National Conference of Catholic Bishops and the Conference of Major Superiors of Men have promulgated the following norms.

I

137. 1. Each institute is competent to admit, approve, and present candidates for the permanent diaconate. Religious commitment to the institute must be made prior to admission to the permanent diaconate formation program. It is the ordaining prelate and the major superior, however, who make the judgment regarding the canonical suitability of the candidate for admission to this sacred order.

138. 2. Each institute assumes the responsibility for the spiritual, intellectual, and pastoral formation of candidates, according to the norms laid down by the Bishops' Committee for the Permanent Diaconate.

139. 3. It is recommended that candidates be trained in one of the centers approved by the Bishops' Committee on the Permanent Diaconate. Each institute, however, retains the right to establish its own program, which would be approved by and accountable to the Bishops' Committee.

140. 4. The faculty given in Article 15 of *Sacrum Diaconatus Ordinem*, for the training of a candidate where no diaconate program is available, also applies to religious ordinaries, Sections I and II of the norms being observed.

II

141. 1. The age requirements normative for this country, as established by the National Conference of Catholic Bishops and approved by the Holy See, apply both to diocesan and religious permanent deacons.

142. 2. Exceptions to this would include such possibilities as an American religious being presented by his ordinary for service as a deacon in a mission territory where there is a lower age requirement; conversely, in international houses, a religious deacon ordained before the age normative for this country might be able to function upon transfer to the United States.

51

III

143.   1. Respecting the competencies of both the local ordinary and the major superior, the current procedural practice for the presentation, appointment, and transfer of members of religious institutes also applies to the permanent deacon.

IV

144.   1. In the restoration and implementation of this sacred order, the ministry of the permanent deacon encompasses both a ministry of service as well as a sacramental ministry to the local Church.

145.   2. All ministries that pertain to the "sacred apostolate" as well as "pastoral and social action" are under the jurisdiction of the local ordinary (*Ecclesiae Sanctae*, I, 25:1). However, it must be kept in mind that "Works proper or special to the institute which are carried out in its own houses, even if these are rented, depend on the superiors of the institute who according to the constitutions rule and direct them. However, these works are also subject to the jurisdiction of the local ordinary according to the norm of law" (*Ecclesiae Sanctae*, I, 29:2).

V

146.   1. The relationship of religious permanent deacons with the body of diocesan permanent deacons:

a. There are important areas of spiritual and professional training proper to the internal regimen and charism of the religious institute which should be fostered and strengthened particularly in candidates for the permanent diaconate.

b. Both the institute and the local Church should mutually encourage the religious deacon to develop the necessary apostolic relationship with his diocesan confreres in order that he might more fully discover and confirm his unique vocation and role within the local Church.

c. There will exist differences in life style and interests between the diocesan and religious permanent deacon. The diocesan deacon lives a dedicated life in the world; the religious has a unique vocation as a member of a particular institute.

d. The religious exercises the diaconal ministry under the authority of the local ordinary and his superiors according to common law; he is likewise obliged to particular law, and directives of his institute (cf. *Sacrum Diaconatus Ordinem* VII, 33).

Cover design
Al Porter Graphics, Inc.
Washington, DC

Typeface
Palatino

Typography
Automated Graphic Systems
White Plains, MD